Return to Gnosis

Knowledge of the Sacred &
What Keeps Us from It

Nick C. Reed

DEDICATION

This book is dedicated to my wise and loving grandmother Janice Lawson who showed me what love is and how to squeeze gold from all I have been given.

TABLE OF CONTENTS

ACKNOWLEDGMENTS

First and foremost, I would like to acknowledge my dear wife and friend Martina, whose encouragement and loving support have been invaluable to the completion of this work.

Second, I would like to thank my grandmother for her tireless effort to make sure I know what love is and has inspired me to look for the sacred in every moment.

Third, I would like to acknowledge Michael Curving who has given so freely of his time, company, editing skills and friendship. I consider myself extremely lucky to have such great friends. Your collaboration has been both enriching and enlightening throughout a number of stages in the writing and publishing process. Our future holds much more collaborations in it.

I would like to acknowledge Luis Garza, my dear brother for the cover design. Across borders and across years you have remained a true blessing and inspiration in the lives of myself and my family.

Further I would like to thank Alex Parker, Caitlin Doyle, John Reed, Paula Marsh, Michael Ninnes, Esteban Flores, Jeffery Groenke, Per Engman, Jeremy Higdon, Rebecca Lee Daniel Valberg and Charlie Yang for their contribution to the publication of this book. I thank you also for your patience in waiting for the project to come to fruition.

I would also like to acknowledge all the others who have contributed in one way or another, directly or indirectly, in the process of this book or my quest. Thank you.

FOREWORD

In reading this book, you will inevitably bring with you the past. Having had the opportunity, pleasure, challenge, and treasure of knowing it's author, Nick Reed, I invariably bring to it my own deeply embedded memories of our personal history together. As I read, I can almost hear his voice as if he were present beside me, intonating the words with a characteristic passion and liveliness of spirit I have come to know so well. I can just as easily envision the glimmer of authenticity in his eyes as though he were addressing me directly. If you too know the author, perhaps you may envision him as I do, or perhaps you will see him differently, according to your own experience.

Indeed, we are all equally liable to carry with us not only the memory of past relationship, but also the conditioning of the culture and traditions within which we have been raised, as well as the knowledge and beliefs accrued over a lifetime of our having read a number of other such books or ancient texts. In this way, the human brain – while a wonderful machine – is constantly evaluating the present in terms of the past, in which case it cannot actually touch the present fully, without feeling it first through the gloves of memory accumulated over time.

To enter into such a state, where one is fully engaged, enlivened by the present and unburdened by the past, is very difficult, or at least, so I have found. It may be synonymous with what is commonly referred to by many today as a state of 'flow' or 'peak' state, and is perhaps somehow related to that quality of transcendent experience which certain mystics have endeavored to convey throughout the ages. In my own life, I have wrestled greatly with the mechanics of how to bring about such a flow.

As Reed notes, "(Man) seeks to flow the stream which carries him, spin the earth upon which he stands, shine the sun by which he sees and would beat his own already beating heart if he could, so that he may live." (p. 68-69)

Through friendship, and in having had many conversations with this book's author, insights such as this have helped awaken within me more fully, the sense in which I've spent a great deal of energy and effort over the course of my life attempting to "flow the stream" as he puts it, and that perhaps it has been something of a miscalculation on my part to have considered the mechanics of it all as residing at the apex of life's journey. The mechanics ought properly to be nested within something more fundamental, of which you may catch a glimpse, as hinted at throughout this book, though not confined to it.

With that said, as you enter these pages within the hallowed halls of your mind, I encourage you to depart from the past. Leave your thoughts and memories of the book's author, and of your knowledge of other such books, and of your accumulated experience of rituals and dogmas at the door as you would a pair of crusty boots. Being light on your feet will make for a better journey, after all, and perhaps you will get a better feel for the landscape. To get acquainted with 'life's truths and mysteries' to which the author so fondly refers, the only real price is a willingness to shed the protective layers of the past and come to it directly, for yourself.

This I believe is the Return to Gnosis to which Reed speaks. It's significance is that of self-knowledge, which lays somewhere beyond the sum total of facts we maintain about ourselves as an identity. For you can't merely obtain such knowledge as you would obtain a piece of jewelry, or other item. It isn't something to be held apart from yourself, to be placed on the mantle, admired from under a display case, or tucked away under your mattress. Rather, it's an openness to a way of seeing, and of navigating life's uncharted waters, that restores a sense of mystery and wonder to living, dare I say even – magic. This is not to say illusion, or the sleight of hand proffered by hucksters and frauds, but rather the true magic and mystery by which the ceaseless stream of life continues to flow itself, and in Reed's words, "that makes all the effort it takes to exist – worth it."

PREFACE

Gnosis is Greek for *knowledge.* In this book, it refers to a sense of things which has become 'Greek' to many. As we move toward more indirect and impersonal ways of relating and interacting, so our knowledge of the world and ourselves become indirect and impersonal. But regarding the knowledge of 'who we are,' 'what is important to us,' 'where we are trying to go in life,' 'what it is all about,' there really is no substitute for the direct and personal knowledge which is the result of presence and participation in life's truths and mysteries.

This book has been written over the course of 6 years. Its brevity is intentional. Every piece has been carefully selected. Every word has been chosen deliberately. You may find the form and style of writing to be unorthodox, but the book is written to communicate something that I believe cannot be transmitted any other way.

There are 26 chapters in this book. There are 26 characters in the English alphabet. Each chapter is intended to reveal a page out of the Book of Life and the character of a sacred language.

What lies herein, is life approached from the perspective of a quest. Along this quest, each moment enriched and added to every other moment; cumulatively offering up something else between the lines. Something sacred to me. The secret I wish to share with you, while knowable, I have found to ultimately be ineffable. Therefor I have written each story, dream, or reflection in such a way that they complement and add to the revelations of every other piece; concealing that certain "something else" – through the sum total of each piece's individual revelation.

This is book is a quest for a grail of a different color. Its reward is greater than any drug on the streets. Its adventure high and challenge real, yet more worthy than that of any movie or novel. Its knowledge –experiential, yet richer and more powerful than any doctoral degree or title could bestow.

This is not a how to, self-help, or divinely-inspired scripture. It is not meant to fix you, make you a better person, install change into you or to program you. This book is not a scientific, religious or philosophical treatise; nor is it a system of belief, political philosophy, or theory to rule them all. This is not a fiction, non-fiction, fantasy, mystery, biography, history, occult, or any other box through which the reader can approach this book with a silo.

This book is my personal mythology and is intended to be read in the contemplative state, not the escapist, or entertaining way in which one consumes a mystery or romance novel. It is meant to challenge you and is written with emotionally charged language to communicate to the heart rather than just the mind. I share these words with you in the spirit that I would share a joke which I have heard a hundred times and now wish to enjoy again through the laughter in your eyes and voice.

This book is not for the person looking for a confirmation of his/her dogmas and creeds, static world views and justifications for having a sense of spiritual superiority or a secret knowledge which will make he/she special. Not for the person looking to escape or be entertained. Not for the person looking to "expose" anyone and everything that moves as being in cahoots with the devil or Illuminati/Freemasons etc. This book is not for the person seeking power or financial gain.

This book is for the person seeking other people's story because they find them to enrich their own, who is interested in what life's truths and mysteries look like from another corner of the universe, who understands that we get much farther much faster together and can learn the wisdom of a thousand lifetimes in one through the company of others. This book is for the person who values tuning their own compass in life.

This book is the echo of the sound of my soul; the footprints of my path. This book is the light coming from a star that may have long since passed and may it spark a fire in your heart for a quest of your own.

1 THE MAP AND THE TERRITORY

This journey began one day when I discovered I had been given a map; the "prescription for the good life" if you will. It is a story you may know all too well.

It is instruction I received on how to "make it" and live "the good life" and it goes a little something like this.

One goes to school to make grades. Makes grades to get into college. Goes to college to get a degree. Gets a degree to get a job. Gets a job to make money. Makes money to buy a house, car, dog, insurance, etc. Oh, yeah, and if you are lucky you can buy the time to *then* do the things that make life worth living.

Yet, I began meeting people who had taken this "prescription for the good life" much further than I had; people who in one way or another seemed to be asking,

"What now? I have everything I need... Did I not get the right dose? .... Maybe I need a bigger house, a nicer car, a better body, another degree, to make more money, status, power? When will I finally be there?"

But the moments which made life worth living seemed to just keep coming fewer and farther between all the other ones.

Already, school had become my map of how to think and what was important to learn, church became my map of how to re-connect, media was my source for the bigger picture, Hollywood became my guide of how to walk and how to talk, and the very poles of my moral compass came to be tuned to whatever was "the law."

These were my maps –which I pored over –hoping they would get me to the place where I was trying to go in life. But regarding the knowledge about where I was going or how to get there, I sat in darkness.

So, on this certain day, where the moments worth living had become an echo of an echo, the shadow of a shadow of my life, I went to the one place left I could think of where I still had a sense of 'who I was' and 'what it was all about.' That was, at the time, surfing.

I must have lost track of time –I paddled out after lunch and now the sun is setting. God, I love it though. Work isn't "work", Pain isn't "pain", nor is tired "tired." Paddling-out isn't some job that must be gotten over with before I can get to the fun part, it is all part of the single sacred act of "surfing."

On the drive up here, I must have been on autopilot because I wasn't even conscious for the latter half of the trip. Out here though, the opposite is true. I am not thinking about anything else, all regrets of the past and worries of the future are washed away and are but faint echoes of this one moment.

It is the opposite of being in a stale room with desks, chairs, walls, fluorescent lights and the low hum of the AC and refrigerator, all of which seem static, dull and un-alive. The constant flux of the ocean surface calls me to keep my balance but also to be awake, alert and alive.

I am constantly responding to the waves, wind and even the sun as I squint with my eyes. Presence is second nature right now.

Paddling out, my only chance to breathe is in between oncoming waves as I duck-dive through them (the oncoming waves). My breathing, the strokes as I paddle, the rising and falling of the waves and eventually everything is beginning to synchronize and coalesce into one symphony of sights, smells, sensations, sounds and spirit.

There is something else though, between the lines. Now in this state, the light in which I see things is changing. Time is becoming dream-time. It is like having a long elaborate dream about brushing my teeth, getting dressed, eating breakfast, going to work, only to wake and realize I had hit the snooze button on my alarm and it has only been ten minutes. Now moments are but one ever-unfolding-moment. Seconds contain entire minutes. The longer I stay out here, the closer I get to finding eternity in each of these seconds, or accidentally staying out here for the rest of eternity as the whole day seems to be passing in the blink of an eye.

It was then that I realized the place where I was trying to go in life: the place where I can say *there's nowhere else I would rather be than exactly where I am and nothing else I would rather be doing than exactly what I am doing in this moment.* If I am to end up anywhere, it better be someplace like this. Why would I want to head toward a place where, once I get there, I would still rather have been somewhere else and doing something completely different? Better to find one moment more worthy of my time and presence than an eternity worthy of half.

During childhood, this was my most natural state. I need not do anything but play. In play, everything was sacred. As I entered adolescence, finding it required diving a little deeper into things. It was found in trying on my new powers. It was to be found in the place where I could lose myself and ironically end up finding myself. "I am the surfer, I am the class clown, I am the fisherman," I would say. But in adulthood, finding this place required a much fuller transformation than I was capable of on my own.

Maybe for others these maps were like a powerful coming of age ceremony filled with millennium-old rituals and rites of passage and was exactly what they needed to get where they wanted to go. But for me they were an insufficient catalyst.

Am I doomed to live on a surfboard surfing every day to have these moments come more often than not? What is it about surfing that I can't get from the rest of my life and everywhere else What keeps me? Further, what keeps US?

These questions though, were not like any to be found in the classroom. They were not multiple-choice or fill-in-the-blank questions, nor would they be answered by any long string of numbers or words or by bubbling anything in on an answer sheet. These were questions of the heart, the nature of which is not a question but a quest.

This was a quest to venture across the spectrum of human experience from the mundane to the complex;

the good, the bad, and all the rest; a quest to take a second look at the activities where we have already found what we are looking for –to see if they might not offer an insight into those parts of life in which life's secret still eludes us; a quest to uncover whether or not that which the legend labels as "out of the ordinary" or "off limits" aren't concealing vast treasures; to see if the parts of the map labeled 'trying and treacherous' don't have their reward and a quest to learn to swim where fools only stand on the shore and speculate because the legend says all drown.

So come! Let us look where the ancients looked! - where all before us and all after us must look for we are not clocks –ticking –waiting to die! Life is not a pointless bloody battle of tooth and nail! It has been a quest from the very beginning towards that mysterious experience that makes all the effort it takes to exist –worth it. To find that, is to find evolution's end. Where evolution ends, is where this sacred "Something" begins, and to know it's mysteries, is to know that strange attractor all life has been developing toward from the start.

2 THE PHILOSOPHERS STONE

I was visiting my grandmother. She always tells the best stories. When my grandmother speaks of her past, you would think she lived the life of royalty. Every story she tells is filled with magic, wonder and humor. I used to wonder what kind of life she had to have lived to speak so highly of everything that happened to her.

Then one day I listened to the actual words; the facts and details of the story and I realized something. She most certainly did not live a life of royalty. That is total bullshit. Her childhood was not all that better than mine. Her parents didn't sound much different than mine. Yet this is really the way she sees it.

The philosopher's stone is a legendary alchemical substance capable of turning lead into gold and giving the gift of eternal life. It is a mythical object capable of transmuting something worthless (or even toxic) into something of great value.

Men have spent their entire lives searching for the stone. Countless books, movies, and documentaries have been dedicated to unraveling the mystery of what this magical substance might have been. Kings, emperors and alchemists have died trying to discover the secret. But when I think of the philosopher's stone, I think of my grandmother and her uncanny ability to squeeze gold from all that befalls her; who with a single story had the power to transform the base metals of her life into a temple for the gods.

What are the stories I tell my children?

RETURN TO GNOSIS

What are the stories I tell myself?
What are the stories I've been told by the millions?
and what is the gold within their breadth?
With stories I build my house,
In which I live till I go,
There are no stories more worthless,
than from them I can't build a home.

3 THE FALL OF MAN

Our history tells of the coming of civilization, the rise of technology and industry, advancements in science and energy, and the development of labor saving techniques. It tells us of the adventures pushing frontiers, the spread of culture, and the birth of great empires, economies and religions. It was a story of progress; the rise of man out of darkness and into our modern world with all its glories and amenities. But contrary to common opinion, history is written by the victors and this story we have all heard is no exception. Much of the world we live in today is not a result of our natural progression as a species nor did it sell itself to humanity of its own accord. It was won the same way the New World was won; through Manifest Destiny and the Spanish Inquisition.

The cultural and social order of modernity were forged in the fires of conquest, colonization, coercion, indoctrination and genocide. They are the result of the entire world having been given the choice either to submit and become a cog to its machinery or ultimately face torture and certain death. The progeny of those who submitted and joined –lived on to be a part of the 21st century. We are that progeny.

If our history were to be told from the perspective of the means by which we have arrived in modernity rather than the ends, it would not tell of the rise of man out of darkness but rather the fall of man into it.

To understand this story, we must first understand another story, the story of the fall of man which the reader is most likely more familiar with. In Abrahamic creation myths, man is also said to have fallen. His fall is the result of eating of the Tree of Knowledge; the fruit of which they say resulted in shame and being cast out of the sacred garden into a wasteland; forever blocked from the Tree of Life. But as with secular histories, sacred histories are often written by the victors and the accounts given to us by the three megalithic religions are just that.

The fall of man herein refers to direct moral knowledge; that is: knowing right and wrong for oneself. Much like our political system, this religious system neither arose naturally nor sold itself to humanity of its own accord. It too was forged in the fires of crusades, missions, conversion, witch trials, heresy hunts, and book burnings, making direct knowledge appear to be the ultimate threat to the powers that be. Having ignorance of what is good and evil is absolutely essential in a world where people carry out acts which are unnatural or unhealthy.

These are not just stories though, they are deep and archetypal myths at the very root of our belief systems today, and their blind acceptance is responsible for the wholesale deterioration of mankind's capacity for moral discernment. Were mankind to ever lose this ability, the intelligence and creative capacity in Homo Sapiens could be unleashed without the guidance of a moral conscience and the world as we know it could be destroyed.

Mankind must regain the capacity to live and learn by presence and participation. Man must learn the value of knowing things directly and the dangers of dependency on a mediating moral authority. Mankind must partake of the fruit of the tree of the knowledge of good and evil him/herself and enter a direct and personal state of knowing, or else mankind will never learn to stand on its own two feet and will continue his/her eternal fall into darkness. His/her rise is contingent upon return to Gnosis.

4 THE DOUBLE-EDGED SWORD

I stand alone in a moon-lit room. All of my family is present in the house, each in their respective rooms, and all is still. Suddenly the moon goes behind the clouds and the house is swallowed by darkness.

I sense a stranger in the house and seek him out. In my hands- a double edged sword. All sense the stranger yet none dare speak of him, for to do so would be to give up their location. But for the moment, we are safely cloaked in darkness.

I hear a sound- my little sister calling for help. I hear my father's footsteps alongside mine as I run over to try to save her. I swing my sword back and forth in the darkness until I hear her body drop to the floor.

My brother calls out for help now- again father's footsteps alongside mine. In desperation, I slash the sword back and forth in the darkness trying to save him but THUD, the body again hits the ground.

Then my other sister, followed by my mother. My father and I alone are left. I swing the sword wild and reckless. No space was left untouched by my sword. Yet he too falls. A heavy and bitter pain anguishes my heart.

The clouds soon pass and the darkness lifts as the light of the moon illuminates the house. I soon discover that there is no one left in the house but the stranger. And in my hands – the bloody double-edged sword.

I'll save you! Says religion. *Without my system of belief all would be Sodom and Gomorrah!*

I'll save you! Says government. *Without my system of control all would be chaos!*

Two sides of the same coin. Two blades of the same sword. One cannot be freed of the freedom of choice. Human nature and freedom are inseparable. To try to separate them is to kill what is human and makes a bloody mess of things.

The enemy is not out there but inside of us. It is our shadow. We are a stranger to ourselves. We want to be saved from making our own decisions; from making mistakes. Yet he who is unaware that his actions are his own becomes a stranger to himself and a danger to others. No one may save another. One by one mankind falls to the double-edged sword of salvation.

5 THE FEATHER OF TRUTH

"He is without blame
Though once he may have murdered
His mother and his father,
Two kings, a kingdom, and all its subjects.
Though the kings were holy
And their subjects among the virtuous,
Yet is he blameless." -Dhammapada

My younger brother (John) brought me to one of his "Best Buddies" events, a companionship program for adults with intellectual or developmental disabilities. We drove together and he told me a bit about it and what they had planned to do during the drive up there. When we pulled up to the front of the building where the event was being held, he pulled over and stopped the car.

"Nick there is something I have to tell you. These people are just the way that they are. You have to just decide before you go in there – whether or not you are going to accept them and love them as they are ... because they can't change and there's nothing you can do that is going to make them be any different."

It was not something totally unexpected for bringing in a first-timer to an event full of people with developmental and intellectual disabilities.

People with such obvious handicaps as Down-syndrome have always escaped judgment and blame in my mind for transgressions. I could never see myself being anything but loving and accepting of them. But people I consider "normal," may at any moment do or say something that sparks my condemnation or blame.

I could no longer reconcile the discrepancy. With nothing but a simple label of the mind such as "handicapped," there became no place in my heart for blame or judgment and yet with a different label, I could justify untold discrimination!

Yet to what degree, I wonder, is the so-called "average person" 100% neurologically perfect, if in fact there is such a thing? And if so what/who would be the yard-stick?

The problem of measuring people's level of intellectual or developmental disability is for me the same problem as identifying a universal age at which people become culpable adults. Children could never do any wrong for "they don't know any better" in my eyes. But for those unlucky individuals who qualify for my label of "adult" the opposite is true.

18 is the magic number," says our society. "17!" shouts our justice system. "21" argues the alcohol, tobacco, and firearm regulatory bodies. Meanwhile other cultures argue, "16, or 15!"

Intellectually or developmentally disabled individuals born in premodern cultures were often revered for their spiritual value to the culture. Here again, they hold up a mirror to my soul and show me the powerful truth of my innocence.

I have heard of the "Kerostasia" of the ancient Greeks, the "Weighing of Souls" of the ancient Egyptians, and the biblical adage from the crucifixion scene, "Father forgive them; they know not what they do." Obscured by their mystical and non-intellectual form, any positive transformative powers these myths and symbols may have once held was lost to the overwhelming taste of religiosity and dogma. That is until now.

"To what degree then," I wondered, "is anyone truly culpable, that is, meriting my condemnation and blame?" And am I not also obscured by my ignorance as a child is obscured by its youth?

In this moment, all the hate, discrimination, judgment, and non-acceptance I have brought into this world, all hate and blame against the Hitlers and tyrants of my day, no matter how seemingly justified, amounts to nothing.

Even this error was itself a transgression for which there stands no merit for condemnation.

All the gears of a great and dark machinery deep within my soul shut down and the Beast of the ages met its timely demise.

Life returned to my veins and warm color to my eyes where once was the dismal gray of untold shame and guilt. My heart weighed fair against the feather of truth, and transgressions I had carried on my own or put onto others shoulders melted as a candle by its flame.

I welcomed a personal symbol carrying the redemptive power attributed to the myths of old. A redemptive experience which came to me not from a religious or political authority but rather a younger brother in an unlikely circumstance, the truth of which echoed throughout all time and space, freeing my heart and my mind from chains I know not I carried. My heart weighed fair against the feather of truth, and transgressions I had carried on my own or put onto others shoulders melted as a candle by its flame.

6 EVOLUTIONS END

It was out of the natural organic life processes that evolution tells us intelligent life arose. Some trillions of years ago, all was caught up in a race to develop stronger claws, sharper teeth and faster legs. That is until at some point, we reached a crescendo, where the legs couldn't run any faster, the body of the dinosaur just couldn't get any bigger nor the claws get any sharper –anymore than the atoms of the sharpest blade could cut through other atoms the same width. Creation, like water flowing forth from a spring –had ran the lush valleys until reaching an impasse. Here, at the limits of our creative capacity, life's creative energy built up like water at a dam; rising like the tide until bursting over its walls; resulting in the spontaneous evolutionary jump to the intelligent life we are today.

So, the limitations of teeth and claws were overcome by the spears and knives, the limitations of legs to catch prey was outdone by the use of the bow and arrow, the defenses of the thickest skins and scales were surpassed by the building of the village wall, and "primitive" spatial intelligence by star mapping and navigation.

Now, we bear witness to mankind's ability to communicate across oceans with only a whisper, peer into space and time without our eyes having become any sharper, split the atom without a knife, defy gravity despite not having grown wings, and travel twice the speed of sound without any changes to our legs. Now we dive to the depths the sea without holding our breath, grow organs, alter genetic codes and replace limbs with prosthetics. We can summon any text, picture, video, or audio ever recorded right into the palm of our hands. With the flick of our fingers, we can create entire worlds in virtual reality and with that same flick of the finger can we push a button and blow up the world ten times over. Never before has so much knowledge and power been within our grasp.

Yet still our greatest medical advancements cannot completely ward off the common cold, the biggest and deepest bunkers and all the drones of the skies cannot secure the next breath and now it seems the very fruit of our creative capacities may indeed be the end of this natural organic order upon which our very lives are sustained.

We find ourselves today in a world that has been so centralized and organized so hierarchically that our institutional bodies again resemble those of the dinosaurs. Through cumbersome bureaucracies, we have red-taped ourselves into a corner and made life itself an unbearable bureaucratic process from cradle to grave –of licenses, taxes, registrations, inspections and fees for everything we do, from being born to catching a fish. We have built up a legal and cultural infrastructure with laws and rules more numerous than the laws of physics; infrastructures which hinder getting our needs met instead of enabling them. Spell check has crippled man's ability to spell as the calculator has done to his capacity to calculate. The capacity to write has been replaced by the convenience of typing and thinking all together has been replaced by 'googling.' Community functions have been replaced by government functions and talking by tweeting. Our environment has become a resource –having no intrinsic value of its own; our brothers and sisters have become human resources and our relationships have become just as toxic as our water and air. The strong and the weak, the rich and the poor, the old and the young, and men and women no longer have complementary roles but opposing ones; where our differences are only found to have significance in the competitive edge or artificial sense of superiority they afford one over another.

It is as if the order has been flipped. It is as if it were to rain upwards and flowers were pollinating bees. Yet it's not the natural world order that is flipping, it's our human world and the stories we write which are backwards.

As once the thickest scales and sharpest teeth could not suffice it seems neither can having all the power or wealth in the world. Again, life's creative waters are reaching an impasse and have long been pooling. It is "intelligence," now, which is reaching its crescendo. But where to next?

I ask because the world is about to be destroyed by the passions and ignorance of the one species capable of real knowledge and playing an active role in how things unfold. Yet the problems we face are indeed human problems, the machinery of which doesn't exist without the gears of each of our participation. The real problem is, mankind has lost sight of what it was all about; that certain sense of things that makes all the effort it takes to exist -worth it, and consequently makes the effort it takes to play an 'active role' –worth it. Thus, we have fallen victim to paths which prey on our passions and follies; paths prescribed by cultural maps and stories which are not only not conducive to our growth, they are in fact our greatest hindrance.

7 LOVE IS THE CHILD OF FREEDOM

We had both gone to Florence alone, she from Sweden and I from the US. It was my Mexican friend Luis who introduced us. But we were only there briefly and just for a single trimester; destined to soon return back to our respective sides of the world; never to meet again.

She wasn't mine, nor I hers, and in fact I saw no point in trying to make it into anything; since the brevity of our stay rendered any such idea an unwise investment.

So, she was free to do whatever she wanted and so was I. And though I never tried to make her mine or to be hers, what we became was better than anything I ever could have made it into, had I tried in the first place.

She didn't have to meet me nor give of time; her company. Yet for some reason she did. She didn't have to say or do anything for me yet for some reason she did and soon I was beginning to get the impression she was doing it not because it was her duty as my gal but because she wanted to. I began to think she was doing it all freely and I had never received love in such a way.

In fact, I found myself doing all of the things that –my entire life –I was expected to do as a duty, but this time it came as natural as breathing, which came quite natural with her I might add.

The brevity of our encounter allowed me a valuable insight. I could see what was right in front of my face without having to lose it and look back in retrospect; seeing what I missed. In that brief time. we shared together, I saw goodness and beauty in her which I so strongly felt the urge to water and grow intertwined. I wanted to care for and protect her; to be there, to give of my all. I wanted to share that goodness with everyone I met on the streets.

I could neither help it nor stop it. I began to notice the life inside of her –in others and in myself! I began caring about my future and health, about the future of others and their health. More for her was more for me, which meant more for others which again also meant more for me and her. It was a win-win situation, the rules of the True Game, and to do otherwise was suicide.

With something so intrinsically rewarding and worthy of my presence and participation, I began thinking about grades, college, career, a house, a job, things my whole life I had been expected to think about and told I should do because it's what I am supposed to…. I now did with the highest reason and most intrinsic motivation.

Like a rip in the fabric of my giant life maps, this experience allowed me to catch sight of the land I traversed… and before the tear could be sewn back up and my eyes blinded by these old maps, I took a look at my life on the land from the perspective of the sea, and lo and behold this wasn't the exception of reality but rather this was the rule.

As I flew home, I saw the trees and scenery out the window as if in a time-scape rising and falling –like drops in an eternal fountain –out of the ground and back into it. Like the waves of the ocean, I saw that my dog, family, friends, and myself included, were all simultaneously coming out of this primordial ocean –into which one day –all would return.

The situation in Italy a perfect catalyst, whereby I now can see what I normally am only capable of seeing in retrospect, after someone or thing had been lost. Here I saw what stood before my eyes without losing anyone.

As our time ended, the experience left not without touching a question already growing deep within the reaches of my heart.

What keeps me from getting what I get from this relationship, from my interactions with everyone else in my life?

When a deer is born, it already knows how to walk. When a bug is born it can take off in the air and immediately fly. But when a human baby is born, it is the most helpless creature on the face of the earth. We must come to "know" ourselves and our world. We relate to our world through learning. "Human existence begins when the lack of fixation of action by instincts exceeds a certain point; when the adaption to nature loses its coercive character; when the way to act is no longer fixed by hereditarily given mechanisms. In other words, human existence and freedom are from the beginning inseparable." Erich Fromm, Escape From Freedom.

For most of my life it seems I have been asleep to the patterns of my cultural genes. That is the myth that people are too selfish, lazy and evil for man to get all his needs met without being made to do so by something. And because of that I subscribed to this game of conditioning myself and others into defined roles; complete with duties and responsibilities are instituted between me and them to keep the world going around. For how else would I get my needs met when I, man, am not an island but need others? Others who are completely free and I know don't have to do or say anything for me at all! How terrifying! To go without love and companionship is to be the last man alive. It is the equivalent of starving, drowning or dying of dehydration for lack of what one needs.

There is power in our needs. When the need for food does not get met it does not go away. On the contrary, it grows stronger and can drive man to do all sorts of things.

So far in history, mans need for autonomy has gone unmet and grown like a tidal wave, coming like a thief in the night, taking many kicking and screaming into revolutions, uprisings and overthrows, only to be replaced again with the new tyrant of the majority. Yet now, in this place and time, I break off my culture as man once threw off his genetic chains and learn to ride the wave in a productive direction, freely.

8 CLASH OF THE TITANS

I got sick. I had a bad sinus infection. I continued to smoke and this turned into strep throat. Then I got bronchitis in my lungs. I smoked still and bronchitis turned into laryngitis and I could not even speak. Finally, the costs outweighed the benefits, and I was miserable. I wanted to breathe and heal.

The sickness lasted for over a month. By the time I was well, I didn't smoke anymore.

I can't say "I" quit because it was more that I was riding on the wave of my sickness. If nicotine was a rip current, I was sucked way too far out to sea to paddle back in. But out there in the abyss, there were big waves. That was how I got back in to shore; riding on the face of a giant.

But there was more to it than this. It was an alignment of my will with that of the deeper me who has wishes to be well; the will of whomever is pumping my heart, breathing, digesting; the one trying to fight the illness. Like the interference pattern of two destructive waves, I had been canceling myself out.

But like two constructive waves, when that deeper part of me became known, my wishes changed, and aligned with those of the one pumping my heart. Then I had strength, momentum, and energy.

There is great power in our nature and in our needs. If my need for food doesn't get met, it doesn't go away. In fact, it only grows stronger. It can drive me to do all sorts of things I would never do otherwise.

My need for health has built up like a tidal wave and taken me by surprise in the night of my ignorance. But now I see you O' Titan and never again will we clash for you I must ride to the shore of my soul.

9 ENTER THE GARDEN

I dreamed that a certain woman and I set out into a garden to make peace. While walking, we came upon a tree and decided to climb up to its peak. Once we had settled onto its limbs, the woman pulled out a Native American peace pipe, and began to raise it to her mouth, when we were abruptly interrupted. A bird that was also sitting in the tree began projectile vomiting right in front of us, in surreal volumes and almost in a cartoon like fashion. We were shocked, saying, "My God, that's impossible. What in the world is going on? Didn't expect that! There is no way we can make peace here."

We climbed up onto a second tree and again she raised the peace pipe to her lips. This time, a bird flew out of its nest and began relentlessly dive bombing at our heads again and again. We tried to swat it away. We tried sitting still, hoping it would just go away on its own. Nothing worked. "My God…" we said, "…it won't stop! We are powerless over this bird. We can't make peace here."

But when we climbed onto the third tree, we became aware that the limbs did not have to hold our weight. Then suddenly from under us, the tree had turned almost completely transparent as did the ground as well. Eventually, we could see out into space in every direction. We had to confront the bitter truth of our reality and let go of control and expectation. We recognized that not only did the limbs not have to hold our weight but that the next time we tried to take a step… the ground did not have to be there under our feet.

As we sat, the limbs did hold, and when we climbed down and stood upon the ground, it held too. This time though, it was a gift. Everything was a bonus to what was granted, for we saw that nothing was guaranteed. From then on with each step we took we knew peace, and set out to share our piece with the world.

There are three trees in the Garden. One challenges your knowledge, another your life. Accept their wisdom and grow in freedom and bliss.

It is not just what people do that is a gift, everything is a gift; every heartbeat and breath. No matter what the probability, it is not certain that the sun must rise again the next day or that the next time we take a step that the ground must be there underneath our feet. At any given moment, there are innumerable different elements involved in 'being alive' which make life not only a gift, but a miracle. This is a truth which we all know intuitively yet the experience which actually makes these statements true is in fact quite rare.

If you were to experience 'life' as a gift, in the same way that you would know life to be a gift if you were being saved by superman from an oncoming train or drowning –then, just 'being alive' would come naturally with such an overwhelming gratitude and wonder –life itself would in fact be intoxicating. It would fill you to the brim with wonder and appreciation that it would overflow and everything we do would be motivated by the desire to express and celebrate that gratitude. From the way that we walk and talk, to the way we relate to and interact with others in society, these mysteries would be reflected in the entirety of our human world.

But life typically does not seem so wondrous that it is intoxicating. In fact, every day more and more people are feeling the need to go out and get intoxicated as an escape because our world is so lacking in any natural sense of life being intoxicating.

We say Jesus the Son of God found what he called The Kingdom of Heaven. We say Buddha the Enlightened One found what he called the Bliss of Nirvana. Yet we believe that this kind of sacred experience is ultimately reserved for a few characters of antiquity. In reality, sacred experience is the birthright of every human being on the planet and yet we are blocked from it as the smoker blocks himself from receiving his precious oxygen by the tar in his lungs.

10 RESURRECTING OSIRIS

I am visiting my wife Martina in Sweden. She goes to class and I go with her to find a gym.

It is snowing outside. The roads are all iced over. I follow her on bike. She would stop at the crosswalk and walk her bike. Apparently in Sweden bikes yield to cars, but cars yield to pedestrians.

We come to one particular street and hop off. She is a little ahead. A bus arrives at the same time. She starts across and the bus begins to turn. They both stop, look at each other, and each again attempt to proceed.

This happens exactly again, and both just go assuming the other will yield.

"Martina stop!" I shout from behind. The bus accelerates into its turn.

She is trapped. With the bus sweeping from her left and with her bike just to her right, she is swept over by the side of the bus and slides right under it.

I can feel the ice beneath my feet. I see none but her and the bus. In this instant, they are one, the entire universe and I are acting together. Arm in arm we run.

Martina reaches her arms out from under the bus and takes my hands. She pulls her legs into her chest quickly and is out. The bus runs over the tires of her bike.

She becomes furious, shouting to the bus driver "What are you doing! You were supposed to stop; there's a crossroad there! It's the law! Didn't you see me?". But I, not being from Sweden, don't "suppose" anything. I am completely out of the loop on how things "should" work over here, and it makes for a completely different experience.

How did my boots grip to the ice like they did? What if I had been just one foot farther away or the bus had been going one mile/hr faster? What if I hadn't come with her today? How did she know to reach her arms out instead of trying to climb out over the bike?"

Wonder and gratitude filled me until I thanked the sun that allowed me to see, the ground that allowed me to run, the air letting me through and the sandwich in my stomach for giving me the energy. I stood at the feet of a world interconnected in ways that I had never seen before making my love for it extend far beyond the sandwich. In the words of a friend, "If you want to make a sandwich, first you have to make the entire universe."

So many pieces have to align, as well as everything that has to line up for these conditions to happen. It is truly a miracle that she is still here with me. Yet it is not just this moment which is happening like this. Every moment happens like this. What keeps us from experiencing it?

I am a man who knows the universe not as it is but as I am. I see the world in fragments because my knowledge of myself is fragmented. The universe acts not as a whole because I do not know myself to be whole. Thus, the world is always either this or that, never both.

Today I stand in a foreign land with foreign eyes to see.

And what I saw through the lines of it all, was 'a world' I want to be.

NICK C. REED

11 DIVINITY IN SYMMETRY

I always thought I was invincible. I had never broken a bone besides a finger and so most definitely was not used to vulnerability. All that changed when I overdid it and hurt my knee.

Within a day, the pain turned into a limp. Within a week, that limp had turned into a hop and before long, the other leg had taken over completely.

Thank God! I have been blessed with another! I thought. Yet this thought was only the surface of a troubling experience stirring in the depths below.

At that very instant, a fuchsia light shined out from the center of my forehead, illuminating the room and making the symmetry of all things stand out to me very strongly.

How naturally the right side takes over for the left. How naturally each eye enhances the sight of the other. How naturally each ear enriches the hearing of the other. Each exists in complement with its other as if it is its highest purpose! Even as I write this, my right hand holds the paper so that my left can transcribe this! I see how every branch, leaf, and root has another root which reaches from the visible and the invisible.

I see that the beginning of the left side is the beginning of the right. The beginning of the top half is the beginning of the bottom. Yet while all sides point outward, it is Symmetry alone which points inward.

What lies on the other side of this mirror old?

"Symmetry" the word, I borrow from education. "Symmetry" the concept, I borrow from education. I have taken many tests and answered many a correct question about symmetry but never have I gasped for air at how all things extend into form through this mysterious portal at the root of all space and time!

An eye for the eyeless and a tooth for the toothless! What Truth! What Mystery! What Symmetry! My soul calls to me from between Its lines. If what I learned of symmetry in those dry dusty ol' books is true, then what madness is this?

12 THE COSMIC MIRROR

*"To see a World in a Grain of Sand
And a Heaven in a Wild Flower
Hold Infinity in the palm of your hand
And Eternity in an hour."* - William Blake

There is a macrocosm microcosm reflection that can be seen from the tiniest atoms which comprise the fabric of material reality to the largest of structures such as solar systems and galaxies. It is a phenomenon which screams "the one in the many!" to us and yet few have ears to hear it. Suicide, war, environmental destruction, discrimination and violence are all examples of our loss of the sacred and the need for initiation into the sacred cosmology.

It is beyond the scope of any book to cover all macro micro reflections thus I would like to briefly mention some highlights in order to illustrate the level of wholeness of our reality of which we live ignorant in our daily traffic and money-making state of mind.

In the ear, a constellation of acupuncture points nervous system of the whole body exist which is a perfect map of the body's nervous system. Each change in the nervous system of the body also has a corresponding change in the fibers in the iris of the eye. The tongue is the same. In the invisible world of electrodynamics, the same torus shaped electromagnetic field can be seen coming from the sun (and all stars), our planet (and surely others), the atom (all atoms), and the heart (all hearts). A very highly sophisticated system in which all fields are but reflections of the one field, evidenced by their toroidal physical properties.

Healers such as the acupuncturist and iridologist have learned (possibly remembered) how to read the microcosms as maps to interpret the macro of the body. They look at the changes in the eye, the tongue etc. for what they reflect of the whole system. Modern scientists and astronomers still stand in disbelief at how the Babylonians had already known our solar system was heliocentric and mapped the planets in their correct orbits thousands of years before Galileo. How the Dogon tribe in Africa knew that the Sirius, the Dog Star, was a binary star system long before western astronomers. Were their eyes sharper than ours? Were they tipped off by the gods? Or does the difference in the way they viewed the cosmos have anything to do with it?

We think of it as being impossible to map the heavens without telescopes, or build pyramids and megaliths without industrial cranes, yet here these enigmas stand against all our prejudice that they should not exist and are a testament to the need for a more holistic worldview. The problem is, to do so inevitably reveals a world that is as alive, intelligent and sacred.

"As above, so below. What is within is also without." This is called the Hermetic Principle. Hermes was the Greek god of wisdom. To the mystics and philosophers of old, the world is the cosmic mirror in which is unique yet a perfect reflection of the whole.

The enigma of the pyramids was not just that it could be built without the tools of modernity. They allude to the very mechanisms used to do it through the proportions of the golden ratio with which it was built. It was a mathematical and aesthetic signature; a universal pattern which they saw repeated over and over in nature from the spiral of a hurricane to the petals on a flower.

The world modern man has come to know could be called the profane cosmology. Man is initiated into a story of the cosmos which is interpreted strictly in terms of its mechanics, bare-nuts and bolts, material, quantifiable, measurable, repeatable and documentable aspect. The qualitative, unique, subjective, mythological aspects are recognized but only intellectually as a phenomenon of minor significance and from which no monetary or real value to life can be derived. Yet even in the mechanical state of existence, in quantum and astrophysics, discoveries have been made which produce paradoxes parallel to what can be found in the ancient Hindu Vedas. The physicist Erwin Schrodinger described wave-particle duality and observer effect with the illustration of a cat in a room with poisoned food. In this scenario, you cannot see inside the room. The question is: Is the cat dead or alive? The answer is both, since relative to the observer they are both real possibilities. This was already expressed by the Ancient authors of the Vedic Text thousands of years earlier. These authors had used the scenario of a pitch-dark room, where the question is: Is it filled with a lush green garden or is it completely empty? Quantum physics and sensitive instruments for measurement were not needed to derive such fundamental truths because of the way they gained this knowledge. An uncontested presence for and participation in the space they occupied in their bodies and immediate surroundings could allow for the enfolding of knowledge into larger and larger patterns or smaller and smaller ones, thus arriving at quantum paradoxes like this.

Our knowledge is a reflection of our relationships and perception of life. We have become divided by everything from the artificial boundaries drawn by our nations to the brands on our shirts. We are divided by political parties, economic and social statuses, football teams and our associations. You can feel this division when you are surrounded by people in a crowd at an event yet cannot help but feel estranged, for although you are all together, there is no real sense of togetherness other than being all congregated in the same place. You can feel it on the bus when people prefer a nice safe spot on the wall to stare at or to fidget on their phone so as not to have to meet eyes with you. You can feel it when you get angry at a car for cutting you off and you speed up next to it to give the driver the finger only to realize it was an elderly person who can barely see over the steering wheel; where faces are masked by tinted windows and communication has regressed to the equivalent of cave man grunts made with our horn as we honk at each other.

At our scale of things, it is through love that we find unity and through empathy and connection that we discover the paradoxes of quantum non-locality. To see myself in you and you in me is to be both here and there simultaneously; a paradox all can recognize yet it is in Gnosis we see Love reflected in the cosmic order.

RETURN TO GNOSIS

Black murky water in a dried-up Creek.
The trees start to stir when the spirit speaks.

An oak stands firm...
With one side burnt...
The other full of leaves on a living-streak.

A wind comes over and a leaf drops dead,
In the black murky Waters and the spirit says.

"Shhhh!" Say the ripples.
"Shhhh!" Says the ground.
"Be still like water for your heart ocean bound."

I hold out this mirror that is my body,
All shattered and spread across the galaxy.
But when healing and knowledge became my
hobby, the picture shown clear a cosmic mask of me.

I am the Leaf Who falls so freely.
I Am the Wind Who moves unseen.
I Am the Oak Who is dying to be living.
I Am the black murky Waters, so it seems..

A star is born by drawing together
What's spirit and matter till hot at the core.
Both heavy as stone yet light as a feather,
For it sits in a space where there is much to adore.

My blood runs cold at the sound of the calling.
My hand unsteady, my footing unsure.
The story I've told is in need of overhauling.

NICK C. REED

The mythical world is no folklore.

13 ANOTHER WAY OF KNOWING

Ages ago, we were all indigenous people of somewhere. Some were hunters-gatherers, others nomadic herders, agricultural, or traders. Indigenous culture was truly diverse yet at the core was a way of life which was simple, close to the earth and with a reverence for the natural world as more sacred than a resource. Their simple, minimalistic way of life is assumed by the vast majority of people today to have been due to being technologically inferior savages but was in fact a conscious choice, and the result of the radically different way that they came to know the world.

Today we have come to believe that any point of view worth considering will take place only in our ordinary awake state and that all perspectives derived from altered or enhanced states are worthless. On an intellectual level, most can recognize the fallacy in this belief, yet few know in their hearts the reality of it for our days are dominated by the money making and problem-solving rush hour traffic state of mind. While the latter state most certainly has its evolutionary purpose, it is better suited for presence and participation in the profane than in the sacred.

Currently, terms such as sustainability, eco-friendly, low impact, recycle/upcycle and natural living are all buzzwords we hear in reaction to our negative impact on our planet. But to premodern man it would seem they were the result of insight rather than hindsight. While today both modern and premodern man would agree that the aforementioned values are not only desirable but ultimately necessary to avoid social, economic and ecological catastrophe, modern man would surely be at a disadvantage to cultivate such values. The problems of treating the environment as a resource and treating people as human resources are one and the same problem: that of relating to the world as an object. An object has no intrinsic value apart from its use by the subject. An object can be thrown on the ground and stomped on and who would think of themselves as an abuser or murderer? So many of our problems share roots in our inability to appreciate the way things are without trying to change them to make them "better." To deny the intrinsic value in a tree, a landscape, a person, a rock, is to deny the sacredness in all things and only recognize the profane.

'We cannot solve our problems with the same level of thinking which created them." Albert Einstein

At the center of native life were rites of passage and shamanic ceremonies embracing dance, trance, drums, chants, vines, brews and sacred plants. The effect of this was invariably a psycho-pharmacologically induced altered state of consciousness. The native way of life was a reflection of the different kind of world they had come to know through the window of these altered states. Their spiritual traditions cultivated conditions extremely conducive to being occasioned by peak level experiences. Their relationship to their environment was simply the natural conclusion from having a radically different experience of self and the environment; making up for what they lacked in quantity with the richness they had in quality.

If you are looking for understanding as to why we see our world as a resource to exploit one need, look no further than our perception of it. We only see the world strictly through the lens of our culturally dominant state of mind. But a world full of resources is no company for man. If you are in a world full of resources you are not in the company of anyone. You are in fact alone. What man seeks is not just survival but that which makes all the effort it takes to survive worth it: call it atonement, communion with the divine, initiation into the sacred, or any other term what fits. It remains that the profane state of mind will not suffice in achieving that. The hole in mans' heart cannot be filled with the profane. Man lives today entirely in an artifact of his own creation. All directions he looks, north, south, east, west, up, down and inward, all he sees is four walls, ceilings, floors, freeways, shopping malls; all he sees is his profane image of himself. Even if he were to transform all the world to his ideals, he would still be alone.

14 THE FALSE LIGHT

When we think of knowledge we most likely are referring to information. Have you ever been asked in passing, "do you know so and so?" How often have you responded "oh yes, I know so and so" when what you really mean is that you know of him/her, possibly just in name or by having seen them in a picture, on the news or in a film. Everything from game-shows to citizenship-tests claim "knowledge" is required, yet questions may be answered using information about the names, dates, numbers and locations and one need never have had any direct knowledge of (or personal relationship with) anything or anyone mentioned.

This kind of knowledge is indeed useful today, and no doubt more desirable than experiential knowledge for we have upon us a context whereby the depth and complexity of life in the 21st century make it seemingly impossible to get by using only what can be confirmed in ones' own life. Entire generations now grow up having been submerged for their entire lives in a world that requires having vastly more information than could ever be gained through direct experience. One needs to be a mechanic to work on a modern car, a CPA to do one's taxes, and a lawyer to navigate the legal system. Countless fields of study and literature exist with more information than could ever be consumed within one lifetime much less confirmed by life.

It is an environment which breeds maps. But when the landscape has changed over time, rivers have meandered, and earth opened up canyons and pushed up mountains, our static maps may lead us on long detours, straight for trouble, or to go in circles for the rest of our lives; digging for treasures in all the wrong places. The real landscape is the living dynamic territory which we would find if only our thick life maps would tear open just long enough for us to peer through and catch a glimpse of its nature, raw and pure.

"Truth" comes from Old Norse trú, "faith, word of honor," modern Germanic treu "faithful" or perhaps ultimately from PIE *dru- "tree", on the notion of "steadfast as an oak" (e.g., Sanskrit "dru" tree). The mind tends to give a sense of reality to things which come to it with "consistency." But what we call knowledge today is more accurately conditioning. For most of us, our knowledge is the result of a form of indoctrination we know by the name of "studying" or more accurately "rote memorization." To achieve this state of knowledge, the disciple repetitively goes over information written "about something" and holds it in one's mind until such time as a test is presented. Although most of what we have learned in this way has never been verified by the disciple's direct experience, nevertheless it bears a strong sense of truth because the information is presented to the mind over and over again with consistency and is held there, 'steadfast as an oak.' This process continues until such a fantastic collage of mental images have been built up that presence and wonder are not only difficult, but completely atrophied, after being under duress for the greater part of the brain's development.

This state of knowing we are so familiar with actually stifles presence and participation. The reader here is invited to recall the not so uncommon moment when their teacher started to present information they had previously introduced. How did the class respond? My guess is that it went something like it did for me, "it's already been covered...." they might say.

The word: "covered," is very accurate here because this kind of "knowing" is indeed covering. Everything known in this manner is covering up some part of the living landscape of their experience with static, dead ideas about it. When something is "known" in this way, there's no desire to give any more presence or participation. Knowledge, in this sense, engenders disinterest, stifles presence, and renders the object unworthy of receiving additional care and attention. But where presence and participation are absent, something will always be left out; or in other words: ignored. And regarding wisdom, which requires a direct and personal knowledge, a deep intimacy with life's truths and mysteries, this kind of knowing is more accurately "ignoring" and this kind of knowledge is in fact – ignorance.

15 THE SEARCH FOR MOUNT ATO

I had learned of a mountain in Sweden. A mountain so sacred that the indigenous only could say of it "that, there" or in the word of their tongue, "Ato." A mountain beyond description, that it could only be pointed at and called "that there?" That's the kind of place I want to see.

I set out on a quest for this holy mountain to see what mysteries it held in its depths.

A colleague drove us. We left at midday northbound for the Arctic Circle; following only rumors and hearsay descriptions of nearby landmarks. By nightfall we arrived at the edge of Sarek, in an indigenous town called Kvikyolk. We meet a native who knows of the place we speak. She tells us we had missed our mark by over four hundred kilometers.

In our bewilderment, my companion backs the car into a pole and is devastated. The car had been entrusted to him by a good friend, he told me. He was almost certain he would not be able to afford fixing it. I knew he would push forward to the end of this quest but would not have been ready to receive whatever this sacred place had to offer.

Our journey changed direction. We set out for Yolkmuk two hundred kilometers east, to find a way to fix the car. There, we found a local mechanic. The parts were not in stock. The cost in parts and labor was much higher than either of us had expected.

The mechanic asked what happened. Upon hearing of our quest and misfortune, he disappeared into the shop. He returned with tools and proceeded to work on the car. We thought he had a misunderstanding due to language barriers and tried to stop him but he insisted.

He labored tirelessly for some time. There was neither a bill nor invoice only a look in his eyes. A truly holy moment. A most unexpected act of kindness. I had chills and goosebumps on my head. I truly stood on holy ground. Who was this man? Why did he help him so? We exchanged eye contact for a moment without saying anything and then we shook his hand and drove off.

We hiked by moonlight and set up camp at the edge of the purple sea. I turned in. When I had fallen asleep, I dreamed I stood at the base of Mount Ato in all its glory. And I had.

16 THE HOLY GRAIL

"A word is like a finger pointing at the moon. It's fine, as long as it draws your attention to the moon, but don't mistake the finger for the moon." -Eastern Proverb.

It is entertaining to think of the Holy Grail as a magical cup containing the waters of eternal life, but I am more inclined to think it is a representation, a symbol for the key to eternal life. The reason the Holy Grail has not been found is not because we cannot find this cup, it is because it is not a cup.

This idea is not new either though. Dan Brown has introduced this into pop culture with books on how the san-greal was a holy bloodline back to Jesus and that whoever has this bloodline is special and guaranteed eternal life. While I disagree with his interpretation, I thank him for popularizing the idea that it could be something other than its literal interpretation.

A Chalice is a strange cup if you think about it. It is a cup with a stem. It is harder to make than a regular cup and the stem doesn't appear to add any functional or practical utility. Grails and chalices are ceremonial and used for drinks with spirit. Would you drink milk or orange juice out of a wineglass?

The stemmed cup is the symbol of inebriation. Much like the Catholic Church's sacrament, alcohol is our culture's drug of choice. But there is in fact a sacrament traditionally used in indigenous ceremonies which is shaped like a grail (and would most certainly predate it) that when consumed frequents mystical type experiences. It is what we call the "magic mushroom."

Known in our culture for its more entertaining properties, this controversial and off-limits living grail was once a spiritual tool used in religious ceremony to produce visions. These visions, unlike those we receive from Hollywood and the media, were visions coming from within and which shamans used in the same way psychotherapists use dreams to gain insight to help the individual on their path of healing or growth.

Mushrooms were highly revered and considered sacred, not for the nutritional value but for the effect upon the soul. It is much more likely the knowledge gained from these mystical experiences was the water of eternal life and the mushroom which carried it was the Holy Grail, not a magic stemmed cup which has been carved in the shape of a magic mushroom.

When I lived in Northern Sweden, I met an indigenous people named the Lapplanders whose cultural traditions paralleled many found in our modern one, yet their traditions were rooted in the experience of sacred knowledge and wisdom.

The Laplanders are the keepers of the reindeer even today, in fact, every reindeer in Sweden is owned by these people according to the Swedish government. While now they have snowmobiles and helicopters, traditionally they were pulled by reindeer in a sleigh. Their shamans dressed in red and white, which are the two colors of their sacrament. Their sacrament is a colorful red and white Mushroom called Amanita Muscaria which grows in symbiosis with the Fir tree and is to be found growing underneath it. The psychoactive compound is produced by heating and drying the mushroom, converting the rather toxic Ibotanic Acid into the spiritually potent Muscimol. Before the oven, I imagine one would hang it over the fireplace in a yurt. This was for them no doubt turning toxic lead into spiritual gold.

Christmas spirit and culture is an interesting phenomenon for this reason. It is a time sacred to many and even magical for some. An elder with magical powers, pulled by a sleigh of reindeer, dressed in red and white and leaving colorful gifts hanging in stockings over the fire and under the Christmas (Fir) tree is a cultural phenomenon wrapped in a lot of mystery both literally and metaphorically.

When someone religious reminds me to "remember what Christmas was about" having made this connection, I cannot help but to think of the Lapplanders of northern Scandinavia and wonder if once upon a time these gifts of the elders would have been pharmacologically capable of inducing mystical grade experiences and the Gnosis of the eternal realms. The only difference between mushroom hunting and Easter egg hunting is one tastes sweet in the mouth but turns bitter in the stomach and the other does the inverse to your soul.

There are also parallels between the Phoenix and the Mushroom. The Legend goes that the phoenix grows from a golden egg, and when it is fully grown it spreads its wings but before it can take flight it bursts into flames and collapses down on itself, to be reborn again out of its ashes. The life cycle of the mushroom reads less familiar though same. It is born into a bulb like ball, grows into the fruit of the mushroom, the head breaks from the stem and spreads flat exposing the gills, and then spreads its wings even convex to form a chalice or grail before decomposing down on itself and rising again out of its own spores.

I imagine the bread and wine of the catholic mass were once not served from mushroom shaped plates and cups but were also mushrooms capable of producing a mystical communion with the divine.

There are a number of highly interesting parallels between the psychedelic mushroom, culture, and religion, and whether that is the result of an unconscious cultural resurgence or a mastermind conspiracy to suppress direct revelation, I rather not speculate. What is of central importance here is that I see religious rituals and cultural symbols stripped of the experience of the things they represent, whether the cross of the church or Phoenix (eagle) of the United States Government seal. Conversations around politics or religion rarely occasion the mystical experiences those symbols represent, but maybe that's just me.

As a child, the mystery in opening a present was within the pattern of consumerism. When I went to church and received communion from a mushroom shaped cup, I wondered where communion with the divine was.

Belief, such as belief in the Easter bunny, was fine as a child, but not if my soul is to grow. I have been stuck in a culturally and spiritually extended adolescence most of my life. Believing, hoping, praying, practicing, and studying. Belief is a cup that is already full. Belief is a room filled with too much light, a blinding and static knowledge. I know not what is really there until I can see more than just my light. The security of adopting a sophisticated system of belief or philosophy has its lure, but what's at risk is having an answer for a question that for me is really a quest.

> *Questions are of my intellect,*
> *Quests are of my heart.*
> *The knowledge I seek is not a belief,*
> *But is the part of my soul in the dark.*

17 THE DEATH OF THE SACRED

I am in a house. Many men stand in a broken circle, each holding a cup half-filled with water. I notice large rings on their hands with strange symbols. The men seem empty and listless.

A small white ball is tossed into my cup turning the water black. A man says to me, "Your water is dirty! Throw it out and get new water!" "When you have done this, you may return to the circle," another said with a disgusted look on his face.

I see it is just dirt and I walk around the room looking for a potted plant into which to pour it. I discover a woman disguised as a man. She wears men's clothing and even a fake mustache. She stands there still and silent, trying not to be discovered.

Behind her is a door. I open it. The door opens to a small dark room. In the room is a pool with a woman floating face up in the water and long dark hair spread out.

"Has anyone checked if she is alive?" I asked.

None answer.

I plunge in the pool. Dark soil streams from the jets, turning the water black. The dark-haired woman awakes and turns to look at me. I get spooked and flee the house.

I am joined by my wife at the road. The dark-haired woman follows me.

"Hey! Don't you recognize me?"

"No." I reply.

"We've been together since the beginning of time."

"Sorry lady, I'm with somebody else now." I replied.

"You'll remember."

We go to the house of a friend from my adolescence. We find him in the garage, readying his truck for the trip.

The air is stale. I duck my head to step out under the half-closed garage door to get some fresh air. As I duck, my shark's tooth necklace swings up and hits me in the teeth. It begins to transform my whole jaw into a sharks' jaw. Startled, I quickly take it off and toss it in the bushes to the left. Suddenly a dark figure runs from behind a tree across the yard to the bushes, then runs off.

I recover the necklace to find a small white skull has been placed on it, about the size of the ping-pong ball dropped in my cup at the house. I feel sad but excited. I put it on and climb in the truck with my wife. We are driven away by my old friend.

As we drive, the dark-haired woman runs alongside the truck, calling to me:

"Hey! Let's take a trip! What do you say?"

"Yea sure, where you want to go? Peru? Somewhere exotic?"

"No. Somewhere much farther..."

I open my eyes as a small child sitting on a counter-top in a messy laundry room full of appliances and laundry. A young girl with dark hair sits across from me. To my right, a middle-aged man leans on a wall looking bored and watching an old TV.

I feel love for the girl. I feel pity for the man.

She speaks with her heart.

"Where are we? Why is it like this?" I ask her.

"You see how we are here?" The girl points at her chest.

"Uh Huh."

"He has come all the way up here." pointing to her head. "He has been in this place a long, long time."

She grabs the phone with her little hands and starts pushing buttons. The man takes it from her.

"Alright… so you want to ask your parents if you can watch the show too I suppose. I can ask…"

He calls someone,

"Hey, can they watch the TV shows? They are getting bored." He names programs violent and highly sexualized.

The man then proceeds to wrap us tight in plastic bubble wrap. We are as swaddled infants. He carries us out. My wife and I pull up in the blue truck driven by the old friend. The man walks up to the driver side window and sets us down on the ground at his feet. The truck leaves and rolls back and the sound of popping can be heard but we do not recognize it.

"Modern man's originality, his newness in comparison with traditional societies, lies precisely in his determination to regard himself as a purely historical being, in his wish to live in a basically desacralized cosmos." -Eliade.

In traditional societies, when youth were initiated into adulthood, they were initiated into their society's sacred cosmology. Their rite of passage marked the death of the profane and birth of the sacred. From that point on, their roles, status, actions and words were given a mythological context as opposed to historical.

Things done by elders even a few generations back had fallen into myth and were described as having been done by the gods at the beginning of time.

Modern man's initiation starts with the disillusionment of Santa Claus, the Easter Bunny and Tooth Fairy etc.... It is an initiation out of the primitive magical thinking and into the new secular order, or Novus Ordo Seclorum. In our culture, the death of myth is a symbol of maturity. Yet myth is not dead to modern man but instead has passed into the shadow of the unconscious where it's powers work mysteries upon us in the dark.

"The Sacred", like "the woman", has been hidden and denied a place in the circle of men and things. Thus, the circle is broken. Cloaked in the myth of the profane, her secrets lay tucked away in the darkest recesses of the heart.

She follows man as his shadow, spooking him with her mystery and unfamiliarity. Her language confuses him for he hears with ears for the profane.

The ferryman readies his boat. Deep and archetypal myths work upon man in the dark. The sacred hides in the shadows of the profane cosmology; scurrying from tree to tree, speaking a language long forgotten.

Why name our children after saints and prophets? Why put flowers on a grave? Why make the beginning of time (0 A.D.) from within the middle of human history?

Man bares her mysteries on his rings, an empty shell of her can be seen in his games, yet know not that her dark waters are none other than the rich soil of the Garden.

The sacred runs because man runs scared. He is driven down this road by a mechanism only the ferryman understands. Her story runs parallel to history. She calls to man from out the window of his secular myth. History takes us forward, her-story takes us back to "the beginning."

To answer her call is to speak the language of the heart. Here, questions and answers come but words will never suffice. When the sacred dies, a part of man dies with it for man is both sacred and profane; both human and divine. When man comes to be only historical man, the only calling he recognizes is the calling done with a phone.

17 PLAYED IN HIS IMAGE

I arrived and went up to my old room. Putting down my things on the chair, I noticed a guitar leaning up against the wall. I used to play the guitar, I thought. So, I picked it up, trying to remember how to play a certain song. It was one of my favorites but I could not recall how it began. Yet as soon as my fingers made the first chord, one after another the chords played and the song come together.

My hands had taken on a life of their own. Half doing it, half watching it happen. My foot began to stomp and the beat was set. My voice added in the vocals and music was made.

Then suddenly I saw something. So, it was with the pumping of my heart. Am I the hand of the one who plays the human song.

Whoever it is that pumps this heart sets the beat, then adds the circulation of my blood, the breath, and cycles of digestion and sleep. And when all this is done and has become muscle memory, the chords of walking and talking and thinking and acting are added and here I am. I am the vocals on top of it all.

Who pumps this heart and who pumps yours? Who sets the beat of every sentient being's course?

Is it the same who pumps mine? Is it the same one who spins the earth and makes the sun shine?

Now I see that "He" is "I", for these chords play themselves, I need not try.

A piece of Osiris, an appendage to the body of Christ, cells in the cosmic body, chords in the music of life.

18 THE ONE AND THE MANY

It is 12:36pm. I study for an exam, alone at my table. A flute plays in the distance. What a perfect time to take five! I break for a brief meditation. I have no idea what is about to take place.

I have tried to be rational and explain what just happened but without question, the gods of rationality just died. They have all found their end in whatever that was. I was not imagining, nor was I dreaming or day dreaming. I was sure I was not hallucinating. Yet what just happened, I am not quite sure. I will account at great difficulty what I have just seen, heard and felt.

What I felt, I can only describe as a 'pebble of pressure' right between the brows of my forehead, about a half of an inch out in front of me.

It was such a strange thing to feel, for I have no pebble organ extending from my forehead, that I could not help but to be astonished. Yet the more I focused on it the more the world around me faded from view and all that remained was this tiny pressurized pebble.

Then the world as I knew it was pouring inside of this invisible pebble until this tiny clear bubble of space became a vast and expansive landscape. The pebble seemed to get larger and larger and the whole world including myself like the hands of a clock swirling backwards, began spinning, condensing and folding in on itself until piercing it and... POP!

It burst! It burst and I was blasted out to I-know-not-where. I was raptured up and out of wherever here is –to –wherever there was; to an infinite degree. It is as if I have been living in a box I hadn't the faintest clue ever existed, only to one day suddenly be thrust through the fabric of that box out to a vast sea of energy. The place was infinitely large, frighteningly open, and free. Yet the whole of it could have been contained inside an atom it seemed. I was everywhere, yet I could not say I really was anywhere at all. The color was black and white, both light and dark, perfectly still and yet traveling through it at the speed of light. The sound was deafeningly loud, yet a silence that vibrated with stillness shined through. There was even a distinct smell, for lack of a better word, of which I have nothing at all to compare. It's reality I could hear, smell, touch, taste, see and still sense in another way yet!

A thousand senses all in concurrence could not have told me where I was. Reality had flipped inside-out. All duality inversed. All opposites were reconciled. I don't know whether I was There or There was Me.

It was an alien landscape yet I felt I had finally, truly come home. The seat of my soul; the ground of my being was here where all was One. Here was unconditional love, freedom without bounds, peace of eternal rest and the bliss of infinite joy.

And I was there when the world flipped back. I surged back into my body like lightning laced with bliss. Energy, love, bliss and freedom flowed through me until I cried. I had not known such powers so pure.

Transformed in ways I was still not sure, I scanned my body with my hands to see that I was okay, and that I was still me. 12:46pm, the clock read. It had been approximately 10 minutes.

Yes, you are once again you, and I am just me; separate out in space, time and 3-D. Everything stands in stark contrast to its opposite. The big was big and the small was small. Loud was loud and quiet was again quiet. Yet all in between, a quality of the infinite remained.

19 AT THE EDGE OF THE GARDEN

I dreamed I am working in a small country diner on the edge of town. I make less than enough to survive busing tables because I have not the presence it takes to serve. A box of fuchsia shirts sits on the floor with our new uniforms for the season. The box reads amazon.com. After work, I walk to my car to leave and am approached by an old friend. She doesn't want me to go. I agree to have one final drink with her before I do so. She wants alcohol. I want a smoothie. The smoothie shop is on the opposite side of the freeway. She tries to follow me in the car but struggles to keep up. I am frequently stopping and waiting for her.

I arrive. I am in a room with no ceiling and only two walls. The walls are tall and made of stone. Moss and ivy grows on them. My wife and a handful of other women approach me. I am speaking with a man about something very important and pull from my pocket a picture of a dog.

He: Is that the dog from the Wizard of Oz?

I: Yes, it is he who pulls back the curtain.

We talk about the subject using metaphors borrowed from books and movies we have in common.

I cradle a woman in my arms. She suckles at my arm. How strange I think that this grown woman being a mother herself would take my arm for a breast. Does she not know that my arm is not a breast? I lead her to my breast. How strange, I thought, that I, a full-grown man, would lead her to my breast, knowing good and well that I have no milk for her? She is not satisfied and tries to eat solids with great difficulty.

In front of me lies a book. On the cover reads, At the Edge of the Garden. What kind of book is this? I wonder, when people ask me from all directions-

They: Infants can't be in the sun. Do you keep it indoors?

Infants like patterns, do you have paintings on the walls with natural patterns?

Have you picked out a good school so that the Infant will grow and develop?

Do you have any infant music? It's good for intelligence.

Do you have any infant books so that it can start to learn about the outside world?

You have air filters, right? So, the infant can breathe fresh clean air?

Do you have a car seat so you can take the infant with you to places? You can't leave it alone.

Did you get immunizations so that the infant's immune system will be strong?

A thousand voices flood my head with tasks all done best by nature, not me. Man strives to be his own father and his own mother yet somehow ends up remaining an infant. He seeks to flow the stream which carries him, spin the earth upon which he stands, shine the sun by which he sees and would beat his own already beating heart if he could, so that he may live.

The Amazon has everything he needs. So, he found the most suitable name for his marketplace—Amazon.com—where everything is but a two-day hike -taken by somebody else to his doorstep, bringing him the image of what was once the real thing. He has cut down the jungle to build a jungle gym. Man's world is an echo of an echo of what was once natural; It is but a memory of a picture of a movie. He talks about the movie and wants to own a copy of it for his collection. His favorite part is where Toto pulls back the curtain on the Wizard of the great city of Oz. He even keeps a picture of Toto in his pocket and yet his world remains nothing but smoke and mirrors.

He wants to leave but lingers for his attachments, unable to leave them behind. Like an infant, with gray hair, we suckle in our ignorance at a tit which cannot give us what we seek. We have mistaken the arm for the breast, and even then, the wrong breast. We do what nature does already, while the rest of our lives go to waste. There is no room to serve when focused on all the things nature already has under control. Our income is not enough to sustain us if we cannot serve and give back. Yet how can we give back if we have not received what we have been given?

Man has dentists to compensate for his love of processed foods and sugars. He has cars in place of legs. He looks without for what is within and within for what is without. I guess we all should consider ourselves blessed that we now live lives two or three times longer than that of the savage, because it takes at least 20 years of doing artificial tasks in an artificial classroom in order to learn to function smoothly in the artificial world man has superimposed on top of the natural world. As early as 5 years of age, children are sitting at desks, doing clerical administrative type work to prepare them to partake in the sacrament of bureaucracy. Surely, this kind of environment will be stimulating enough to cultivate in them the attentiveness and presence they need in order to serve. It is more likely though that they will become a waste and stuck cleaning up the resulting waste of their ignorance.

With books for eyes, man stands in his ignorance at the edge of the garden, wandering lost in his wasteland, suckling at the teat of a dusty rock. It is we who are the faithless ones, who sense the fruit but who dare not eat of the tree on which it grows.

But a room with no ceiling and only two walls, no matter how tall, is no room at all. It is a passageway. It is our orientation which faces us with a wall in front of us and a wall behind us. The passage to the garden remains unobstructed.

These walls are teeming with living moss and ivy. Look around you! You are not in a cage. You are in the Great Halls and Chambers of the Kings of old! Every book you see and picture in your pocket is leading you along its corridor. You may effort to flow the stream which carries you yet never the less you are ocean bound. Let your breath rise and fall and your heart pump itself, how and why is not important to this mystery. What is important is that you receive the income of one who is a server.

20 THE TREE OF KNOWLEDGE

"...And so it goes that people either love the tree and hate its fruit, [or] love the fruit and hate the tree". Coptic Gospel of Thomas.

Mystery in our times starts with Santa Claus, the Easter bunny and the tooth-fairy, and has become associated with falsehood and non-reality. When something's a mystery to us, it is either a form of entertainment or due to a lack of education. In fact, what we find in our educational system is a situation where being in a state of mystery could mean not passing a test, and ultimately not passing over into adulthood. As muscle is built in the gym and not on the couch, so knowledge requires mystery. And while many would be quite content to live in a world without mystery where all the universe conforms to their static maps, mono-cropping destroys the soul.

Birth, coming of age, marriage, parenthood, elder-hood, sickness and death conceal great truths and mysteries. It is a mystery that no two moments contain the exact same constellation of people, places or events. It is also mystery that each moment is in many ways a reflection of every other moment. The truth is that all moments are but one moment; unique yet familiar, knowable yet mysterious, fleeting yet eternal. The truth is also that each moment seems more one than the other.

All that is known comes from having presence and participation in That which is unknown. Mystery is a garden in which the tree of knowledge grows. It is not eating of this tree which has cast man out of the garden, it is his discomfort with the unknown which blocks the way back with flaming swords. To re-enter the garden, one must become comfortable with life's truths and mysteries. And to live in the garden, one must more than become comfortable, one must again become a steward of the garden. Man must become the Light which moves through the Darkness of the unknown with the ease of a child at play. Conversely, to deny the unknown a place in one's life is to deny the light of the stars passage through the night sky. And to deny that part of oneself that sits in darkness is to deny that part of oneself which shines the sun and spins the earth on its axis.

"The fool who knows he is a fool is that much wiser, but the fool who thinks he is wise is a fool indeed." -Dhammapada

----

Man has light inside of him. Man has darkness inside of him. Each man contains darkness for each man contains parts of himself which he denies. Truth is a bright light to behold, too easy is it to look away. Know thyself and behold the Light of one's soul.

Who among us can enter the garden? Who can strip off the rags of dogma, charge into the darkness of the undiscovered Self as the light of a star? Who will become a keeper of the garden wherein the tree of knowledge grows? Who will taste the fruit of freedom and bliss?

21 KING KARMA

I stand in the apartment of an old friend, Esteban. It was a small apartment with an open room just as you enter, with a kitchen off in the back. I greet him and a young lady over by the kitchen. He seems anxious. The air is stale and thin. I dare not ask. I hear cars pulling up and people getting out quickly and abruptly. Esteban's face told me everything I needed to know about what was about to happen. Karma.

"Sorry, not my problem!" I said as I ran out the back door. I wanted to help my friend. I wanted to save the damsel in distress, but not as much as I wanted to get the hell out of there. After all, it wasn't my karma.

I jump over a fence and land in someone's backyard. A dog chases me and attacks my leg but I hardly noticed having been in such a state.

I find a closet-like room in a little shed out back behind a neighbor's house and hide myself there. I bury myself under clothes. Suddenly the door slides open, it is a boisterous woman shouting loudly and oblivious to approaching Karma.

W: "Hey! What are you doing in here?"

I: "Shh! They will hear you! Come in quickly and keep your voice down."

She comes in but continues to make a lot of noise. She doesn't understand. The door opens and a single shot sounds off. The neighbor collapses while grasping her heart. I scramble to rebury myself but I am too late.

I now face Karma out of sheer necessity. Karma is a large and intimidating character with a large gun in his hands pointed right at my heart. I quickly thrust my arm out in an attempt to divert the gun away from me. What an impossible task, I couldn't possibly keep this up forever.

I: "What are you after me for?"

Karma: "Esteban's past."

I try to keep out of the line of fire.

I: "Why me though? I am not Esteban, am I?"

Karma: "Oh you are most certainly Esteban."

He shoots me in the chest. I fall to the ground, like I am supposed to, you know. What will happen next? I wonder. When should I die? When will he leave? Will I get to watch him walk away? Will I hover over my body for a while?

But I do not die. And Karma does not leave. He surprisingly stands there and continues to shoot me over and over again. What madness is this? To beat a dead horse. But then again, I am not dead as I had supposed either. The pain is overwhelming. I get up and run away in pain but unhindered.

Looking back over my shoulder, I see Karma. He has no mercy. He is headed directly into a school. Now even the innocent will feel his wrath. I change course and now pursue Karma.

I: "Please, they are not Esteban! They have nothing to do with him or his past!"

Karma: "Oh but they do."

This time I am shot in the stomach. I teeter there for a second before falling; I wish to fall backwards onto the flat ground behind me. The steps look painful. But if I were really shot, how would I fall? I think, and so I fall… hitting my head on the steps, just like I suppose I should.

When will the teachers notice me and run over frantically shouting and panicking like they are supposed to? Just then, one of them turns her head and sees me. Three teachers come running and begin to examine my wound.

Teacher 1: "Oh my God, he is shot!"

Teacher 2: "Is he dead?"

Teacher 3: "Hey you two, look at the hole in his stomach, doesn't it look like another naval?"

Teacher 1: "Cool! It is!!"

The teachers play with their fingers in the gunshot wound in my stomach until finally I have had enough. Having become irritated, I sit up and put an end to this madness.

I: "Alright that's enough! I am not dead, OK?

Startled, they all look to me for explanation. I have none. I am confused myself as to how and why. What am I to do now? I wonder. So, I stand up and throw my arms around people, shouting "I'm alive! I'm alive! Can you believe it? After it all, I'm still alive!

I ran to a mall from my childhood to find people I knew whom I could celebrate with. I ran in and shouted "I'm alive, I'm alive!"

I stand there in the corridor of the mall. People pass me on either side. I am dreaming, I realize.

A rainbow light shines out from the center of my forehead, illuminating the whole corridor and making everything and everyone appear super vivid and ultra-real. Am I dreaming all of this? But it all looks so real, more real than I have known in my waking experience.

An Indian man passes by from my right. I grab him by the shirt with two hands:

I: "How does it feel to be a character in my dream?"

He: "I don't know, it is just like anything else."

I was expecting to be able to predict his response. I did not. Is this real life? How could I not know what he would say to me? I went outside to get answers. I try to fly. I fly over the grass first, just in case I am not dreaming. I landed head first on the concrete on the other side of the grass with a "crack" in my neck. There was a sharp pain. No way I am dreaming. That was too real.

I walk to my car. The key is in the door but the door lays on the ground. That's not how it's supposed to be. What is it doing there?

Just then, Karma pulls up in a SUV with guns drawn.

I zig-zag to the mall. Windows burst with Karma in hot pursuit once again. Around and around the mall we go. I run until I cannot run any longer. I hide in my coffin but know that Karma doesn't care and will find me either way. I confront Karma once again, taking the gun and shooting him. Light shines out of the gun and turns him into sand. I feel relieved momentarily but the sand gathers back together. I try to disperse the sand but it is no use. Again, I find a gun in my face. I try to dodge bullets, pleading, "Why me, Why me? I'm not Esteban!"

Who am I? Am I Esteban? Why does Karma follow me?

You are Esteban, the believer in Karma. You are the Karma who chastens you. Let you awaken yourself. Let the light of knowledge fill the corridor.

Your legs are heavy with delusion. You bury yourself in fear. But nowhere can you hide from yourself. You are carried life to life upon your supposed-to's and supposed-not-to's. Yet as long as you slumber, you remain asleep at the wheel of Samsara where Karma is king.

When dreaming, the one who is awake is the one who realizes that he is dreaming. When awake, the one who is dreaming is the one who does not realize that he is reality-ing.

Energy cannot be created or destroyed, only changed from one form to another. There is death after life and there is life after death.

Death is not the end and the truth is not what you think it is before you have come to know it in the light. You are the dreamer of your dream, even if you do not know yourself enough to recognize it in your responses.

There is emptiness in reality. There is reality in a dream. Each person brings out a different side of you. Each person shows you a part of your soul. Deny that they are you, and they will not be you. But neither will you be yourself. Ignorance is a bright light to behold but favor the dark and watch as you slip back into your slumber. See truth as truth. See ignorance as ignorance. Arise. Escape the King of Karma.

22 THE END GAME

I was flying out of Stockholm airport. It was 1am and I was trying to find a place to get a bite to eat while I waited. I found a 711 on the bottom floor and bought a sandwich. As I sat down I noticed a man off in front of me sitting at a public computer rubbing his eyes. He was sitting up on a tall stool next to the wall. There was a couple sitting off to my left, reading magazines. By the time my eyes had made their way back to the man in front of me, he was in mid fall; tilting back on the tall stool and headed towards the ground.

He hit his head on a radiator on the way down and then landed with a thud on the floor. I ran over to help him up asking if he was okay. He nodded and said he was, though he clearly wasn't. Strangely though, he didn't seem as worried about his fall as something else that seemed to be bothering him. In Spanish, he just kept saying over and over again, "what am I going to do, what am I going to do?"

I didn't know what was going on but he looked weak so I asked him if he was hungry. When I asked, he looked up to me and tears began to stream down his cheeks. I bought him a sandwich. He ate it with the paper and everything. I wondered what was going on so when he had finished I asked him his story.

He was a Colombian who had come to Sweden with the hopes of making enough money to send some back to his family, offering them a better life than he could from Columbia. He had planned eventually to

75

save enough to move his family here with him some day. That day was 5 days ago. Over the years his wife had left him and it was just his daughter coming. His daughter was going to meet him at the airport and he was going to sell a man two laptops as well, making enough money for food, room, and a bus from Stockholm to his town. When he arrived in Columbia, neither his daughter nor the man showed up and he had spent his last dime on the laptops, an unfortunate gamble. He said he stayed in the airport where no one would help him and no money for 4 days. On the fifth day, all he had was his return ticket so he returned to Stockholm where he again stayed without money to return to his town. He said he had asked for help and even tried to sell his necklace or the laptops, but he was accused of pan-handling and was thrown out in the snow. It was mid-January and far below freezing in Stockholm so he said he snuck back in to try and use this public computer to contact a lady who he rented a room from in his town but he had no luck. He said he hadn't eaten in 5 days and that was why he was so hungry he did not care about the paper. And now he doesn't know what to do because he is stuck here. Except, it wasn't he who was stuck, it was us.

I wondered why no one had helped him. Out of the corner of my eye I saw the couple looking over at us. I walked up to talk to them about helping the man. Oddly, they began looking on their phones for "which department of government might handle this situation," and when they couldn't find one they said sorry, they couldn't help him. I realized I had done the same thing in walking over to them; passing the check. So, I decided to break the pattern. I found out the bus times and how much it would cost and proceeded to find an ATM to pull out some money to give to him. I put my card in the ATM and pushed the buttons and BAM, I realized why no one had helped him.

As I pulled out money I realized, I wasn't doing so well financially myself, and every dollar I was giving to him, I took one step closer to being there; in his position; where no one is going to help me because then they will be one step closer to being in my position and so on ad infinitum. It was a vicious cycle; a rat race and in it, the rules of the game made generosity –suicide.

To act as you would have others act; to do as you would have others do, to treat others as you would have others treat you. How is this such a radical idea when these words have echoed through the chambers of saints and mystics of old for centuries? I wondered. And yet so it was.

What good could I do to break the pattern, I wondered, when I am just one person and nobody else changes? But as I looked around I realized the whole world simultaneously thinks the same thing. And so, generosity has become the divergent act of a radical.

Most who I tell this story get hung up on the possibility that he may not have been telling the truth; that I could have been deceived. And they are correct, I could have been deceived and there is no way for me to "know" because I do not know him personally nor do I know anyone to ask who knows him personally and whom I trust. There is no substitute for direct knowledge and personal relationship. Yet I did what I did because of the direct knowledge and personal relationship I wish to build and inspire, not because of that which I had with the man.

"Sorry I can't help, I can't find what government agency there is for this sort of thing." These were my words just a few hours before this. This man speaks my language. Because of my lack of trust, I placed my trust in control. Poverty and misfortune was a political rather than a community issue. I would have rather chosen to send this man to a government agency where the penalty is steep for lying. Yet it is in control I have placed my trust, not love.

One might think that government is a substitute for the lack of community; that government agencies have replaced the roles people in community once held such as evidenced on its face by the man who passes the check to government agencies for even the simplest acts. But community is not dead. It has merely changed form. What we have is a community of control; a community where personal relationship and direct knowledge are not only not valued but are not trusted.

We have a culture where nobody knows anybody and therefore doesn't know if they can be trusted, thus everybody opts for control systems to fulfill community functions and everybody opts for control systems to fulfill community functions and therefore nobody ever gets the chance to have direct knowledge that someone is trustworthy through first-hand experience and personal relationship.

He who values becoming a trusting person as much as having trust and he who values becoming a generous person as much as depending on the generosity of others does more for a community than

a thousand fully funded government programs for
their gift is the kind community they inspire.

23 THE HOLY WAR

It was rather late at night and I was on the road. I pulled over at a gas station and went inside to pay. Two cops stand at the coffee machine off to my right.

"What are ya'll doing out so late?" I ask.

"What are you doing out so late?" One replies.

"Fair enough"

I finished paying but something inside of me compels me to go over and talk to them. I walk over towards the coffee machine and start a conversation.

"Hey, so how is you guys' night going? What's it like working the night shift, is it busy or is it pretty chill?" I ask. I hoped to simply connect. But I got no reply. Well, at least not the reply I was hoping for.

"Take your hands out of your pockets. Is that your car outside there? Is it registered in your name? Do you have any ID on you? Where are you headed so late?"

One of the officers, the younger one, began to tremble a bit as he talked faster and faster and then something inside of me again compelled me to ask him…

"People don't come up to you, do they?"

"No, they really don't." The younger one replied.

"Is this weird for you?"

"Yes, this is very strange indeed. Very strange and I'm not sure what your purpose is and until I figure that out I'm going to need you to step outside with me."

I am now being pushed out a gas station door into a dark parking lot by two angry men with guns, that's how I saw it at least. One corners me between two cars while the other goes to his patrol vehicle and runs my plates looking to see what Uncle Sam has to say about me. Then I realize the opportunity.

"Do you want to know why I came up to talk to you?" I asked the older officer.

"Sure, tell me."

"When I hear a siren calling and red and blue lights flashing I don't want to feel anxiety and defensive even when I'm doing nothing wrong. When I see a man in uniform with a badge and a gun I don't want to see a cop I want to see a human being. When I come up to talk to you and see how you are doing I don't want you to see a suspect or a trouble maker. I want to see a human being. I find that as I grow older the circle I draw around myself keeps getting smaller and smaller and the people I identify with and can trust are getting fewer and fewer. When everything I say and do can and will be used against me, I don't want to say or do anything. Yet in a world where I have not the trust to say or do anything then nobody has the knowledge to help me either and I might as well be alone. There is a war going on. Yet the war is not the war against cops and it's not the war on the American people. The war I am talking about is not the war of the 'us against them' but the war of us against the whole idea of there even being an 'us against them.' And I want you on my side of this war."

24 THE GREATER JIHAD

It was the year of 2011 and the height of the Iraqi Insurgency and War on Terror. I am living in a small town in Sweden attending a language school for foreigners. As I walk through the halls of the building, I hear a voice call out to me from the far side of the building.

He: "Hey, you are from America, no?"

I: "Yes", what's up?

He: "Hey, what do you think about Obama? Is this a good or a bad man, huh? What do you think?"

I: "Never met the guy, really can't say."

He: "Yea but come on, what do you think… Isn't it true that on American TV all they show is bad things about Muslims? Muslims blowing things up, you know, suicide bombers and those type? What do you think about Muslims, are these good or bad people?"

Within 30 seconds he had started a conversation about both religion and politics, in a very polarized way. But I also saw something else. Regardless of its form, he was defending something sacred to him. And though I couldn't prove it, I was beginning to trust my intuition.

I: "Damn man can't we just be people today? Look, I don't want to get into this kind of talk because I have to be either left or right and you have to be either Muslim or Christian etc.… Either way I go there is always the fence; always the false division. Then you are on one side and here I am on the other."

I show him with my hands. "People are people. Not fun this way ok? When you come up and talk to me from now on" I take his hand, "I want you to talk to me like am your brother. Though you may not know this yet, we are brothers."

He stands there and crosses his arms. The man looks back at his friends behind him and when he turns his head back to me he looks me in the eyes and tells me, "that is how I want to be with everybody," he says, "I don't want to be seen as a terrorist because I am from Iraq. That is just one extremist group. I wish more people were open and like you. Like family."

Abdullah invited me over for dinner at his house. We sat on his floor. He had no furniture or even a table. His family had been killed in the war. He fled to Sweden. I was the only person he had ever met from the US. All he had known was what he had gathered from Iraqi TV and news showing US soldiers in acts of violence against Iraqis. We talked late into the night sharing our stories, learning and understanding eachother's differences, seeing each other as people; as family. The encounter was one of the most profound encounters ever and the original setting made it to be so. As the light shines twice as bright when coming out from behind the clouds, so too the false divisions and separation between us made for an even more powerful impact. To expect to find a white devil and end up meeting ones' family, is a sacred moment.

Your soul is spread out across the void. If only you were to realize your void; your emptiness within yourself then you could draw your soul together.

Pull yourself together as a star does when it is born. Only when you are whole will you be a light to another.

I am not the Nazi. I am not the terrorist. I am not the cop. I am not the judge, the globalist, the materialist, the banker, the corrupt politician, the scrupulous CEO. I am not the stupid, lazy, evil, ignorant, powerless, and slavishly dependent. I am not the rapist, the murderer, the child molester, the cannibal. I am not him, I am not her!

So, we tell ourselves. And because of this we can never be whole in our microcosmic being for our soul is scattered across the macrocosm of humanity.

Man grows in outward knowledge but this story prevents inner growth and wholeness.

Man may cut his hair and shave his beard and pluck his feathers to resemble the face of the good and the clean, but the purpose of the bathroom is to address mans' dirty and otherworldly side. Forsake a bathroom and man shall watch the playing field level in favor of his other side. Then what shall he see when he looks in the bathroom mirror this time?

Strength and resolve come from having a molten core. Compassion draws together the stars many elements until they warm. Once man warms up to the idea that inside of him exists all that he denies presently, he will find his resolve.

Where is man's mother? Where is man's father? They are always "there." Find "there" and find the father and mother. But find "here" and find yourself.

When "there" becomes "here" then will man's mother and father become "you."

But you walk a path which is not your own. Your elements are scattered; pulled apart by the space between you and all those you swear you are not.

Where is "there?" It is every pace you swear "here" is not. Heaven is a "there" and hell is a "there." Never a "here."

You say "the afterlife" for the same reason you take short breaths. Breathe in the whole of the "here" and "there" you will be.

It is the lazy meadow which takes your breath away and it is the lazy meadow which makes for the roughest passage through life. Unlucky you have been to be born in a life which makes "being good" so easy for you. Maybe in the next life you will be born to a corrupt power family or robber or addict and will have the opportunity to meet the rest of yourself.

It is the meadow which keeps you. True, once upon a time you used to hate all things "good and pure" and loved all things "evil" but always you have been one or the other and never both and thus you never seem to get "there." Eternally you have remained a child dependent on an external mother and father.

"When the two become one, and the inside is like the outside, you will enter the Bridal Chamber." Coptic Gospel of Thomas.

Learn where "there" is, so that elsewhere may be sought here and now. Breathe deep into the fullness of empty space. Pull yourself together. Integrate yourselves when you meet them and you will find the resolve you need to shine and be born among the stars.

25 THE WORTHY PURSUIT

There is a hole inside of mankind's heart; it is a bottomless pit of infinite depth which lies inside each one of us -a hole of which no measure of quantity will ever suffice.

Everyday modern man tries to stuff this hole with food, degrees and accolades, friends on Facebook, money in the bank, power, status, image, and the rest. But let us consider, even if one of us were to finally possess all of the power, knowledge, and wealth of this world, would that even be enough? Where then is the missing wealth to come from?

We turn on the news and hear of the consolidation of wealth out of the hands of the many and into the hands of the few, growing social injustice, environmental destruction, war, domestic violence, prejudice and ignorance. Yet the greatest ignorance is in not recognizing the opportunity for the purposeful life.

I once was invited to sit in a Utopia think-tank. We sat around the round table to share our vision of Utopia.

"No more war, no more hate, no more starvation, no more inequality, no more illness, no more pain and suffering, no old age or death." When it was my turn to speak I could only describe the world I saw when I looked out the window. What would I have to bring to the table in a world where nobody needs anybody anymore? What would I have to offer to a world that has everything? What would be the value of life?

Today we look out the window and see the world lying in ruins and past the point of no return. Yet who among us can look out the window and hear a calling? Who among us has eyes to see a pursuit so meaningful, so worthy that one would pursue it even if they knew they might fail? This is truly the kind of purposeful life we dream about in fiction and fantasy books and movies. We love to see our favorite actors and actresses rise to the occasion; how, with a single mind and a whole heart, they break from their bondage, and overcome all barriers against all odds. We revel in how there is no amount of discomfort, effort, wrongful accusation, or threat that deters their heart's steadfast lock on the worthiest pursuit a fictional story-line could produce; pursuit which we are starved for.

Never in the history of the world has there been a greater need for this kind of individual, for the whole world says simultaneously, "But I'm just one person!" And nobody does anything.

Let us stop for a moment, and ask ourselves: Are we clocks -ticking -waiting to die? Or is there something more… hidden perhaps… just between the lines and beyond our present interpretation of things? Could there be something great we are missing, something which we might discover if only the thick fabric of our giant life maps would just tear open long enough for us to peer through and see life -raw and pure?

The question is not, how can I escape the unbearable reality of a life not worth living? Rather, the question is in fact quite the opposite. What is a pursuit worthy of my fullest presence and whole-hearted participation? How can I overcome those things which compel me to remain unalive, so that I may live fully? "And not" as Henry David Thoreau wrote, "When I come to die, discover that I had not lived."

We spend countless hours in dark hypnotic theaters watching actors act out what real purpose and calling look like in a fictional scenario, yet the setting for the worthiest of pursuits lay hidden within the fabric of this moment, and we know it not.

26 THE BEGINNING

"The disciples said to Jesus, *'Tell us how our end will be.'*

Jesus said, *'Have you discovered, then, the beginning, that you look for the end? For where the beginning is, there will the end be. Blessed is he who will take his place in the beginning; he will know the end and will not experience death.'"* -Gospel of Thomas

I lay in the snow, staring at the cloudy night sky. Who am I? What am I doing here? Where did I come from? Where am I going? The clouds part and a meteor comes ripping through the atmosphere; streaking across the sky. Then, just as suddenly as it had come, it vanished.

Then it hit me. I have no idea where I come from or where I'm going after I leave this world, but while I am here, I'm going to light up the sky!

And to how many more eyes could I bring magic and wonder than that of the meteor?

ABOUT THE AUTHOR

Nick C Reed is an author, speaker, social-entrepreneur, activist, surfer and modern mystic who constantly works to spread passion and the sacred side of the world. Presently, Reed lives in Austin, Texas with his wife Martina and daughter Jessica where he consults, coaches, and provides wilderness based rites of passage/coming-of-age programs for youth and adults in the community.

What is the story you have heard growing up? What are the maps you have been given?

Where is the place where you can say that there is nowhere else you would rather be than exactly where you are in this moment? What is it that you do that you can say that there is nothing else you would rather be doing than exactly what you are doing in this moment?

What is a pursuit so worthy of pursuing that you would do it whether you succeeded or failed?

What keeps you from getting what you get from you most intrinsically rewarding moments from from the rest of your life and from a calling that answers a real world need?

Where have you yet to find the sacred? Who can you not see in yourself?

If you were to die right now and look back in retrospect, what would you not have known you had until it was gone?

Once you have secured your survival, what makes all the effort it takes to exist worth it? And further, to take an active role in making the world a better place worth it?

Who are your heroes/heroines? What are the traits and characteristics they exhibit which you admire?

What end of the pole are you on? Young, old, strong, weak, man, woman, rich, poor, etc...? Where is the opportunity for purpose?

Where do you lose yourself, and simultaneously find yourself?

Where is the sacred in each of these 26 chapters? Where is the sacred in yours?

If you knew that after person you meet that you would never see them again, what would you say to them? What would you do for them differently?

What is your comfort level with mystery and the unknown? Where do life's truths and mysteries elude you?

What is your story and what gold can be made out of it?